Carl Larsson's Home

Pictures Karl-Erik Granath

Text Ulf Hård af Segerstad

ADDISON-WESLEY PUBLISHING COMPANY Reading, Massachusetts ● Menlo Park, California
London ● Amsterdam ● Don Mills, Ontario ● Sydney

Library of Congress Cataloging in Publication Data

Granath, Karl-Erik, 1918-
  Carl Larsson's home.

  Translation of Carl Larssongården.
  1. Larsson, Carl Gustaf, 1889-1959. 2. Sundborn,
Sweden. Lilla Hyttnäs. I. Hård af Segerstad, Ulf.
II. Title.
ND 793. L26G713 1978   759.85 (B)   78-15503
ISBN 0-201-07698-5
ISBN 0-201-07699-3 pbk.
ABCDEFGHIJK-FEAL-798

United States edition, 1978, distributed
by Addison-Wesley Publishing Company, Inc.

ISBN 91-970070-2-1
©Granath & Hård af Segerstad Förlagsproduktion 1975

Produced by Granath & Hård af Segerstad Förlagsproduktion
for the Swedish Booksellers Ass.
Translated by Pearl Lönnfors
Designed by Bertil Samuelsson

"That small house, lying bare on a heap of slag. True, there were a few enduring small birch trees and a few lilacs, as well as a potato patch.
But I called it my own.
Off and on, and with small extra savings, Karin and I, with the help of the village carpenters, blacksmith, bricklayer and painter, prepared a bit here and a bit there."

As simply and humbly as that was the beginning, in 1889, when Karin and Carl Larsson installed themselves in the house, called Little Hyttnäs, in the Sundborn village, part of the province Dalarna in central Sweden. In two short decades they came to change, extend and decorate it into Sweden's most well-known and most beloved home of all times. The house was received as a gift from Karin's father, Adolf Bergöö. It belonged to his family, and two of his sisters had lived there. This very usual wooden cottage of two rooms, kitchen, attic, entrance hall and woodshed on the North gable, grew during the years of "replenishing" into a considerable building complex. But it never became large, it never lost its intimacy or its human dimensions. While room was added to room and space to space in the most unconventional way, Karin and Carl built in all the comfort, warmth and joy along with all the other qualities, so obvious yet so difficult to capture, which have made Little Hyttnäs into the home above all others for innumerable persons.

The quotation in the introduction is taken from Carl Larsson's autobiography. It was formulated more than half a century ago, but the description is valid in all its essentials, even for people in the society of today. It confirms the timeliness, which explains the striking and growing interest shown nowadays in the Sundborn home. Karin and Carl Larsson felt a need, along with many others, for a compensation–dwelling in the country, by all means small and embedded among summer's birch and lilacs. Like the rest of us, they had limited resources and not a great excess of time. Carl Larsson was not only a great artist, but as such also an impressive worker. Therefore, at least in the beginning, Little Hyttnäs grew at intervals and with the help of extra savings, and naturally in close cooperation with the sturdy tradesmen of the village. This occurred at a time when the city dwellers of the commencing industrial society had to learn to regard the representatives of the genuine handicraft trades with admiration and respect, to be sure somewhat romantic. Gradually Carl Larsson painted an impressive series of portraits of his handicraft friends of Sundborn. Last but not least, Carl Larsson confessed in the leading quotation how he, the once poor city boy, felt being able to call the small house on the heap of slag his own. With Karin and Carl Larsson's home, a Swedish and Nordic summerhouse ideal was realized at an early stage. It was gradually transformed into a permanent residence.

Today Little Hyttnäs is officially called Carl Larsson's Home, situated in the Sundborn village. Most of us have an image of how the place looked and how they lived there during Karin's and Carl's time, thanks to all their famous books. The striking thing about it now is that the "home on the sunny side" has been preserved to the minutest detail and that it lives on, not only in the sense that growing numbers visit it every season, but also in the more proper meaning that it is inhabited at times, especially during summer and winter holidays, by the now rather numerous offspring of Karin and Carl along with their dear ones. It is certainly a noteworthy house which still functions splendidly after seven to eight decades, with no changes other than the modernization of the heating system and the hygienic facilities.

That all is preserved with such piety, as it once was, is the presupposition for this book. We can here, for the first time in coloured photographs, document all the well—known surroundings of Carl Larsson's Home.

Whoever visits the house in the village of Sundborn or looks through the pictures in this book and is captured by the idyllic and harmonious character of this home, should keep in mind the environment in which Carl Larsson grew up. During the middle of the 19th Century Sweden was what we would call today an underdeveloped country and Stockholm, a small capitol with typical poor neighbourhoods. Carl Larsson's description of his growing-up environment, in the distressed Stockholm, is shocking, and we have double reason to regard with admiration and respect his restless eagerness to fulfill his aspirations despite the social handicap. The poor boy became not only Sweden's leading monumental painter of all times and a brilliant illustrator, even viewed internationally. As the "sunshine man" and the painter of homes, he came to occupy a place in the consciousness of the Swedish people as no other artist before or after him. Earlier I called the Sundborn home a compensation—dwelling. Against the implied background, this denomination becomes justified in its deepest meaning.

This is not the place to touch more closely on Carl Larsson's artistry, but it should at least be said that his thirty years at Sundborn were far from always marked with the bright mood that flows towards us from the many home pictures. His wrestling with the great artistic tasks, with the depressions, illness and setbacks of the later years also affected the daily life at the Sundborn home.

Karin Bergöö had a completely different background. She came from a well-to-do home, which besides was so liberal–minded that she was allowed to educate herself to become an artist. Karin and Carl met in the village of Grez, outside Paris, and were married in 1883. They were both internationally–oriented youngsters, and this view towards the rest of the world, which was not so usual for Swedish circumstances at that time, grew wider and deeper during the course of their marriage, thanks to their many voyages. Besides, Karin had a married sister in London. This contact came to mean a great deal in the forming of the Sundborn home. The truth really is that this so "Swedish" home would never have been realized without Karin's and Carl's impressions from Berlin and Vienna as well as Paris and London. Whether or not Karin was together with Carl on these trips, they kept in close contact with each other by uninterrupted letter writing. We know that this intimate unity, which so strongly marks their correspondence, had a decisive significance on Carl Larsson's artistry. Of course it also played an import role in the forming of the home.

We talk about Carl Larsson's Sundborn, but this is naturally deeply unfair towards the untiring wife and mistress of the house, Karin. Not even their children can describe without ambiguity the division of work in decorating the home, but there are strong indications that the peaceful, mild and thoughtful Karin contributed quite as much as her impulsive, inventive and artistic husband. And mistress Karin's contribution surely was not "only" that of the practical housewife. She was not an artist herself for nothing, and you need not stay long in the home before you notice what her woven or embroidered textiles, at the same time refined and distinctly patterned, contribute to the whole.

"How small everything is here." This is said to be the most usual comment among visitors to Carl Larsson's Home. The remark has many meanings. Above all, you compare Carl Larsson's paintings and drawings with the actual interiors. He often painted the rooms in a frontal, very deep perspective, which made them look larger than they really were. In other words, he made use of what in modern camera technique is called a wide-angle perspective. Surely one of the reasons for this was that in so doing he could capture more details and render the exploration more meaningful.

The second reason why visitors find "everything small" is that the rooms actually are small. Both the diningroom and the entrance hall each measure only 5×5 metres. This modest scale naturally enhances the impression of cozy intimacy, and the visitor's comment, therefore, always carries an undertone of enchantment. We usually like what is small and cute, and we are pleased that this famous home hardly is larger than our own. A not so minor part of the popularity of Carl Larsson's Home can probably be explained by the fact that it appears—contrary to the grandiose artists' homes of the times—so encouraging to everyone who either owns or is dreaming of a summer home. Everything has a liberating simplicity. Even the straight—forward carpentry appears reproducible by a somewhat skillful amateur, to the extent that it meets with the requirements of today's building inspectors. Carl Larsson would have been the first one to appreciate this kind of recognition. He was hoping that his example would be followed by others and liked to view himself as a teacher in the art of making oneself cozy and reasonably comfortable with small means.

The method of building room after room onto an existing cottage, so that the house practically "wandered" across the lot, probably originated in England. Karin and Carl knew it well; they were generally familiar with the renewing of dwellings in progress at the time on the Continent, above all in Austria. English architects such as Voysey and Baillie Scott, their Scottish colleague Macintosh, as well as the Austrians Olbrich and Hoffmann were among the outstanding men of the time, in this field. They liked to use simple rectangular forms, stylized decors and a colour scale of green, rose and yellow against white. This is not the place to analyze these relations, it should suffice to point out their existence and that those interested can find room interiors in the English trade literature of the time bearing resemblance to the drawing-room of Carl Larsson's Home, even to the point of confusion.

The main annexes to the original log house were built in 1890 and 1899–1900, but even in—between some minor changes were made, and a carpenter could almost always be found in the house. In 1890 the first studio was built. It was placed along the front of the house beside the entrance hall and facing the diningroom and drawing—room, leaving the windows towards the studio, though the diningroom window was altered and painted. A rather large open fireplace in the studio, with a high, white English-type chimney made it possible to heat, as well as lending a picturesque accent to the exterior.

For reasons easy to comprehend, this studio was not particularly undistrurbed, and in 1900 Carl Larsson inaugurated a larger, detached studio, at an angle to the North part of the house. The earlier studio was then transformed into a type of family room, where Karin could sit and sew or weave and the children do woodwork or play. The room was rechristened the Workshop. The following year the family moved to Sundborn for good. In order to prepare room for 11 persons, the old woodshed at the North gable was torn down, and in its place a two—storied extension of the original house was erected. On the ground floor of the new addition was a pantry, a washingroom, a maid's chamber, a boy's room and a bathroom, while on the upper level was a reading room, a guest room—the so—called Old Room—Suzanne's room, wardrobes and a dressing—room. In 1912 a cottage with beautiful paintings was bought from Aspeboda. It was attached to the studio and at the same time an upper and lower Dovecote were built in under the high roof, as summer rooms for the children.

When Karin and Carl Larsson created their home at Sundborn over two short decades, they were in unity with the best endeavours of their time. Simultaneously they succeeded with something so unusual as to have enrichened those endeavours in essential aspects. Their home became unique and exemplary and has so remained. Seen in a proper international perspective, the home is unprecedented in Europe and a vital part of the culture at the turn of the century.

Since 1943 the buildings are administered by a family society. Despite the increasing flow of visitors and the frequent private use by a growing family, you find the interiors as cared—for and fresh as during Karin's and Carl's time. The floors are newly—scoured, the flowers healthy, the textiles ironed with care and a summer wind is playing with the sheer curtain hanging in the open window.

"Welcome to this house, to Carl Larsson and his spouse". No word of welcome in Swedish has become as known, famous and beloved as this one. It is printed in fine artistic writing with a merrily uninhibited mixture of styles, above the entranceway to the Sundborn home, against an embellished background and framed by borders of flowers and leaves. Actually it is a kind of instruction for using this friendly, generous and, in all aspects, open home, the key to an attitude towards life.

When the Larsson children rowed off on their "viking cruises" along the Sundborn River towards the South, they could see their home from this perspective. To the right is the pale red drawing–room and bedroom wing while in the middle of the picture is the white–washed studio building, placed at an angle. To the left, with the blue railing, is the brewery which has now been redone into a summer lodging. The high red building seen in the background, though, is not a part of Carl Larsson's Home, which is situated close to the other town buildings. Originally the white fence ran along the length of the shoreline to keep the children from falling into the water. The picture is taken in early spring. During the summer Carl Larsson's Home is embedded in a thick green foliage. On this page is the enfenced boat dock. A glimpse of Swan Island can be seen in the background.

Carl Larsson's Home is situated like a little crowded village at the bend of the Sundborn River, with water on two sides. The plot is not large but there is room for quite a few small buildings, which were used earlier as a brewery, a bakery, quarters for the servants, a fishing shed, a woodshed, a stable, a garage, a food storage and a cold storage. They were readily at hand but at the same time the arrangement is unforced. On the left is a gable of the earlier stable, and below the upper part of the well, decorated in a rural Empire style. On the opposite page is a lodging with a starling's nesting–box and a characteristic weather–cock.

The rear of the main dwelling reveals a care—free mixture of building techniques with the most varying features. On the left is a log wall running outside the dining-room and Carl Larsson's bedroom. Around the window is a nailed—on decoration, painted green, which was attached some time between 1906 and 1909. On the facing page you see that the same log wall outside the diningroom and bedroom is covered with a reddish—yellow wood panneling which probably occurred between 1903 and 1906. The little flower—box, which was on the log wall, was nailed in place again outside the drawing—room window. For some unknown reason Carl Larsson had the original East wall of the log house, outside the kitchen and reading room, plastered, which probably occurred before 1906. Therefore it may be difficult to discern the division between the log building and the new addition to the right. It is most noticeable with guidance of the different roof heights. In order to break up the monotonous impression of the plaster surfaces Carl Larsson had a basically—red edging nailed on. This type of mixture of materials and styles was not uncommon around the turn of the century.

To the right of the boat dock you see the yellowish–red panneled gable of the original house, with the long drawing–room window and the little bedroom window. The wind–breaker of the built–on original studio, the present Workshop, is uniquely wave–shaped. The high white chimney located in the facade is of an English villa–type. English influence can also be traced in the new, white–washed studio building on the left, with its tin roof. The long, low window lights–up the hallway into the Studio.

All kinds of decorative, often drastically humorous, ornamental details can be found in several places in Carl Larsson's Home. The blue fantasy bird sits atop the Workshop. You can see figure–shaped consoles carved in pine under the roof, among them a self–portrait of Carl Larsson, ''which with outspread nostrils would sniff in all the winds, and which would stare out towards land and shore''. The front–door landing was originally built–in, but was opened in accordance with the traditional rural style. On the right–hand wall, above the fire extinguisher cabinet, Carl painted, in 1891, portraits of the children, Suzanne, Ulf, Pontus and Lisbeth, in a four–leaf clover.

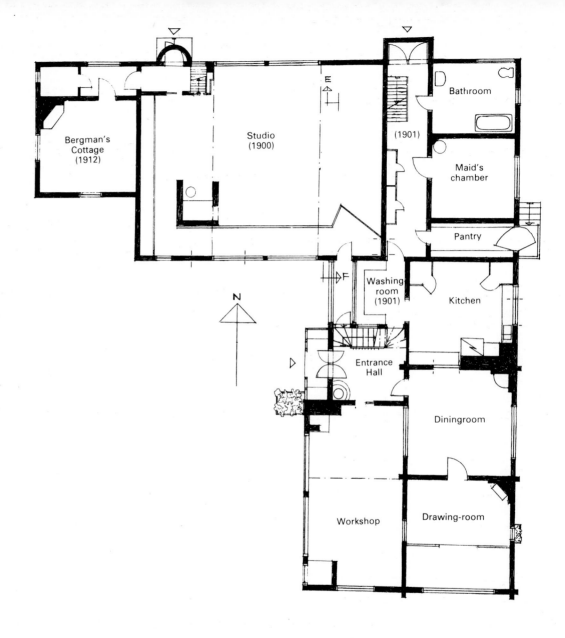

Bergman's
Cottage
(1912)

Studio
(1900)

(1901)

Bathroom

Maid's
chamber

Pantry

E

N

F

Washing
room
(1901)

Kitchen

Entrance
Hall

Diningroom

Workshop

Drawing-room

Lower Level

Entrance Hall

In summer 1890 the first studio was built, the present Workshop. At the same time a rather large open fireplace was constructed in the corner of the Entrance Hall. This also resulted in the possibility of installing heat in that small but important entrance room. In a letter to Karin, Carl wrote, "If you have enough money, buy an iron stove. In one week I'm coming with gold in my pockets, of course". This faithful little heater is still standing in its corner under the shelf with the wooden vessel, which Karin and Carl received from their painter–friend Anders Zorn, and which they valued so highly. The Entrance Hall is painted in a warm, welcoming colour scheme. The open–work metal lantern which appears in Carl Larsson's drawings is still hanging from the ceiling. Of course it was originally meant for a tallow candle.

"You stumble into a little entrance hall where you will have difficulty finding a place for your overcoat among all the children's wraps", Carl Larsson wrote. Each member of the family had his own hook on the staircase at just the right height for children of different ages, two hooks for the parents and seven for the children. The saying about the little mirror on the stairpost is: "Look into the mirror at your own pleasant face". If nothing else, you notice the two clothes brushes on either side of the looking–glass. On the left of the picture is the hallway into the Studio outside the washingroom. The picture above shows the stairway's "stile", photo-graphed from the hallway to the Studio facing the entranceway and the stove. On the opposite page is the door to the Diningroom, diagonally ahead, to the right of the Entrance Hall. The gong is used to gather the scattered flock to meals.

Workshop

Let's first take a look at the Workshop. This was the first
studio, which is why there are so many large windows,
the longest facing the yard. From here Carl Larsson could
actually look out in all directions: towards the yard and
the river, into the Drawing–room and the Diningroom,
into the Entrance Hall and if he so wished, into his own
bedroom through the opening below the ceiling. On the
opposite page is the Northeast corner of the room with
the painted window towards the Diningroom, and the
door out towards the Drawing–room, with the wonderful
portrait of Karin. "On the sliding door I've painted my
idol… That sofa pilar. That's my paint cupboard. Rather
cunning, with slots and names for the colours. Sitting on
top of it all there's an old man, carved by carpenter Berg-
ström from my drawing". To the right are Karin and the
drastic caricature of the master of the house.

The picture of the large portion of the Workshop is taken from the left window of the Drawing–room, which opens up between that room and the Workshop. Outside is seen a glimpse of the lodging. On the left, before the red pilar, there is a little podium where Karin used to have her sewing machine. While she sewed, she also kept an eye out on what was happening in the yard. Comfortably within reach was her weaving loom. In the picture below is the now old–fashioned crank sewing machine, on which Karin tirelessly sewed all the children's clothes, fantasy costumes for all sorts of pranks or historical attire for Carl's paintings.

This is the window between the Workshop and the Drawing–room from which the picture on the previous page was taken. The contrast between the bright Drawing–room, with its lighter and more delicate furnishings, and the darker more robustly equipped Workshop is typical of the Sundborn home. Practically room after room was added as the need for space arose. At the same time, Karin and Carl tried out new interior ideas and paved the way for new furniture- types as well as useful and beautiful objects, brought back home from their travels. They did not allow themselves to be bound by preconceived opinions, but at the same time they were forced to keep within the range of rather limited economic resources for quite awhile. Below is a crocheted potholder on the wall facing the Entrance Hall.

The picture on the right shows the Workshop wall facing the yard, with its long window in the direction of the small podium with Karin's sewing machine. On the folded drop—leaf table is one of Karin's tableclothes with its daring and effectful simple pattern. The picture below shows a very characteristic detail of the house. The green wall pilar with its shelf actually conceal the former outer corner between the Diningroom and the Drawing—room and is therefore a part of the outer West wall of the original cottage.

The open fireplace in the Workshop is located in the corner towards the Drawing—room and can be described as a combination of English and Swedish. However, the decorative, curled—up cat on the hearth appears to be typically Carl Larsson. Coming to the picture on the facing page, we have completed our wandering around the Workshop and find ourselves again in front of the sturdy sofa fixed to the wall backing on the Diningroom. Here you can see the paintings on the window somewhat better. Originally there was a motif from the Middle Ages with a castle, a knight and a maiden, but in 1905 Carl Larsson repainted it. What is left of the Middle Ages is the castle and several floating angels towards which Karin and Carl turn their well—known pro-files.

Diningroom

CL and KB = Carl Larsson and Karin Bergöö is embroidered on the runner, for its time daringly artistic and assymmetrically composed, on the scrubbed oak leaf of the long table in the Diningroom. We begin with this picture in order to emphasize Karin's important role in the decoration of the Sundborn home. Even the weaving which can be seen in the background on the high—back sofa is composed by her, as well as the majority of the many textiles in the home. On the opposite page is a more unusual picture of the Diningroom, with the specially—built shelves for the encyclopaedic work, *Nordisk Familjebok,* which Carl wanted to have at hand when some obscure point had to be cleared up during the lively dinner discussions. Even Dickens used to be kept near by: "If the soup was too hot, the *Pickwick Club* was pulled out, and was read a-while until we didn't have to blow on our plates any longer."

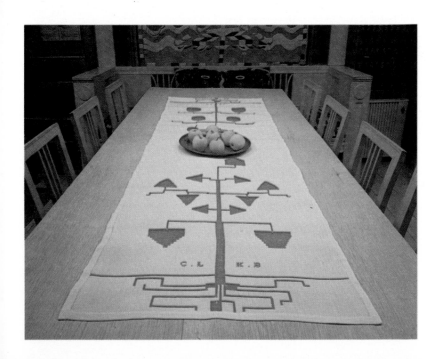

The Dingingroom is the commonest motiv in paintings of the Sundborn home. Although refurnished and changed many times its basic character is strikingly unaltered. Remaining from 1894, the time of the first Dingingroom pictures, is only the china closet beside the door to the Drawing–room. The spindle chairs of 18th century Gustavian style were ordered from carpenter Arnbom who made them for 3 crowns each. They are upholstered with natural–coloured leather cushions made by a shoemaker. Karin had Arnbom put up the panelling on the walls but waited until Carl came home from a trip before chosing their colour. The green of the panel and the yellowish–red tone of the shelves and furniture aroused intensive discussions among those interested in interior decoration at the time. Karin had a long shelf put up along the walls for all the small objects that her collector–husband brought home. The porcelain bowl in the smaller picture is one of those humorously decorated by the father of the house himself.

The lamp shades in the Diningroom are Carl's own design. They are cut out of stiff paper and have been strikingly likened to blooming cactus flowers. "… and the spindle sofa is rumpled in the Carl Larsson way", writes the father of the house on one occasion. Notice that the slats in the backrest of the sofa have been given a bend which reminds us of the slatwork in the Drawing–room, but otherwise the sofa is most like an old weighty Swedish high seat. Karin's textiles play an important part in the context. The cushion with the flames symbolizes World War I and gives a dramatic accent to the milieu, unusual for this home.

During one of the years just after the turn of the century the door between the Diningroom and the Kitchen was closed off in order to get rid of the smell of food and the rattle of dishes. The shallow space between the door posts was used as a storage space for cigars and Sunday dinners' "little nip". It was named the Sinner's Closet. "Karin doesn't like that but I think it looks honest and respectable", Carl confessed. Below the closet is a practical half–circular drop–leaf with room for a beautiful tureen, for example. According to the custom of the time, Carl was inticed by proverbs and had the cry of the French Revolution, "Liberté, Fraternité, Egalité" printed above the Sinner's Closet and on top of that the milder "Love One Another, Children, as Love is All." There is a portrait of his son Esbjörn on the door to the Entrance Hall with the challenging sentence above it: "I Tell You What: Be Glad and Good."

On the left is a close–up of the bookcase with the Nordic encyclopaedia. Notice the simple unartificial carpentry. On the opposite page is the North East corner of the Diningroom facing the door from the Entrance Hall. The curtain arrangement of a short white valance with sewed–on cloth loops instead of rings was one of Karin's specialities. In front of the pewter platter on a special shelf is an old timepiece with a chainweight which ingeniously can hang through the shelf. The window of English type takes up the curved form of the slats in the backrest of the sofa. On the whole, the lighting of the Diningroom is subdued and friendly. Cozy security and cheerful warmth are nearly ideally united in this room .

Drawing-room

If the Diningroom is dark and cozy, then the Drawing–room is light and cozy, a Gustavian sunshine room, blue and white, as the sky and the light passing clouds, with reflections from the glittering water through a friendly window. Here, if anywhere, we stand in the Swedish summer room with its permanently just–scrubbed wide floorboards, white, Gustavian–style chairs–inherited from Karin's aunts–sheer, starched curtain flounce and other textiles in matching colours, everything from the durable carpet runners to the chair covers, with their gathered flounces, to the tablecloth designed by Karin. The discreet graphic art on the walls complements but does not compete with the central picture of the room, the view towards the water, the islands and the forest, framed in thriving ivy.

The Drawing—room window is now, as during Karin's and Carl's time, filled with flowers, and in the middle there is usually one of the wooden vessels that the family received from Anders Zorn and which Carl Larsson often drew and made use of as vignettes in his books. The Drawing—room podium with its white balustrade is a successful loan from turn-of-the-century England. Originally the podium was no longer than the window sill but it was extended a few years after the turn of the century when the railing also was added. Under the small window facing eastward Carl Larsson painted one of Jean Erik Rehn's murals. The magnificent tile oven, manufactured in Falun in 1754, was found by Carl in an out-house "where it was mashed together into a pile with a fire—hole". Out of joy over his find, he allowed the flowers on the tiles to bloom out onto the ceiling in a radiant bouquet. He was one of the pioneers among the enthusiasts of the time who began to take notice of the importance of preserving what we had left of old objects.

On the door between the Drawing—room and the Diningroom Carl Larsson painted a portrait of his happy bright—eyed daughter Brita. The door in the large picture is open in order to give an idea of how it looks when you leave the Drawing—room and go from the light room to the darker one. On the left you get a glimpse of a secretary, at which Carl used to sit and attend to his correspondence, while the youngsters romped around him. The drawing—room, you see, was a far cry from the fine room which someone might expect to be inspired by upper class furnishings. On the contrary, it was to the fullest extent a family room, with activities ranging from doing homework to drinking coffee, when you could not sit outdoors but still wanted to feel close to nature. Even the dog was allowed here and liked to place himself as a "lazydog" on the podium, where Carl on occasion used him as model.

Here is a last glance of the Drawing–room with a
section of its fourth wall, the one that faces onto
the Workshop. Seeing the window in the middle
of the wall, you have the illusion of looking out
into open space. But the Workshop lies between,
and the dim outline of the red outhouse appears
outside the long, vertical garden window behind
Karin's loom. To the right is the previously mentioned secretary. The picture on this page shows
a close–up of the copied landscape sketch by
Rehn, mentioned in another context.

Studio

To the Studio you can go either through the door on the North side of the building or from the Entrance Hall over the earlier—mentioned "stile", along the passageway outside the washingroom and through the door with the old magnificent lock, shown here as an example of the objects of historic interest which Carl Larsson so early understood to appreciate and preserve. Just inside this door is a small nook called the Holy Corner where Carl Larsson collected a few objects inherited from his poor childhood home. Between the two vases is a little porcelain bowl which was used when Pastor Pettersson christened, in Sundborn, all of the Larsson children in one rather extensive ceremony, in which the entire ritual was repeated for each and every one of the seven offspring, and the baptizer, with a sigh of relief, finally took on the youngest, who was of a more normal format for such a ceremony.

The long passage from the Holy Corner behind the Studio screen is overflowing with art of the most differing kind, often gifts from artist friends, an album of paintings which tempts exploration. On the left we see the view over the yard and towards the front–door landing through the long window, which earlier let the South sun into the Studio, before the wall screening out the light was put in. Just at the end of the passageway, where you turn to the right into the Studio and cast a farewell glance through the last little window out towards the yard, the contours of a statuette stands out against the foliage and the arch–shaped balustrade of the boat dock. It represents Carl Larsson's Financier Pontus Fürstenberg in Gothenburg and is modeled by Per Hasselberg.

DILIGENT AND FULL OF HOPE
DO FIND YOUR TOIL MODEST.
THE SUN RISES IN A FRIENDLY WAY
SHINING ON HARD WORK.
REAL PROGRESS, ADDED PEACE,
MORE JOY IN LIFE.
AND YOUR OWN COMFORTABLE HOME
WAITING 'ROUND THE CORNER.

"That rhyme stuck in my mind once when, as a
little rascal, I happened to see it in a book of
verse beside father's razor, which I meant to
sharpen my pencil with", wrote Carl Larsson.
That little morality in verse came in due time to
be printed in beautiful capitals as a border
around his large studio at Sundborn, at the time
the biggest in the country, measuring 9×12 metres. Today the Studio nearly gives the impression of a church hall with the memorial altar in
the center, from which the bust of Carl Larsson,
sculptured in granite by his friend Christian
Eriksson, standing between two fine candle-
sticks of turned ore, stares intensely vigilant at
the visitor. Behind him, at the back of the hall,
Stockholm's Ladugårdsgärde spreads out in the
"School Children's Choir"–the cardboard model
of a fresco for a school in Stockholm–formed as
a tribute to the youth of Sweden. In the background is the part of Ladugårdslandet where
Carl himself spent several of his poor, difficult
childhood years. On the right of the picture is a
sketch for the decoration of a girl's school in
Gothenburg. To the left is a figure–study for
"Wet of Midwinter", his much debated and finally rejected suggestion for the decoration of the
National Museum's stairwell. The Studio was inaugurated when the little church of Sundborn
rang in the new century, the year 1900.

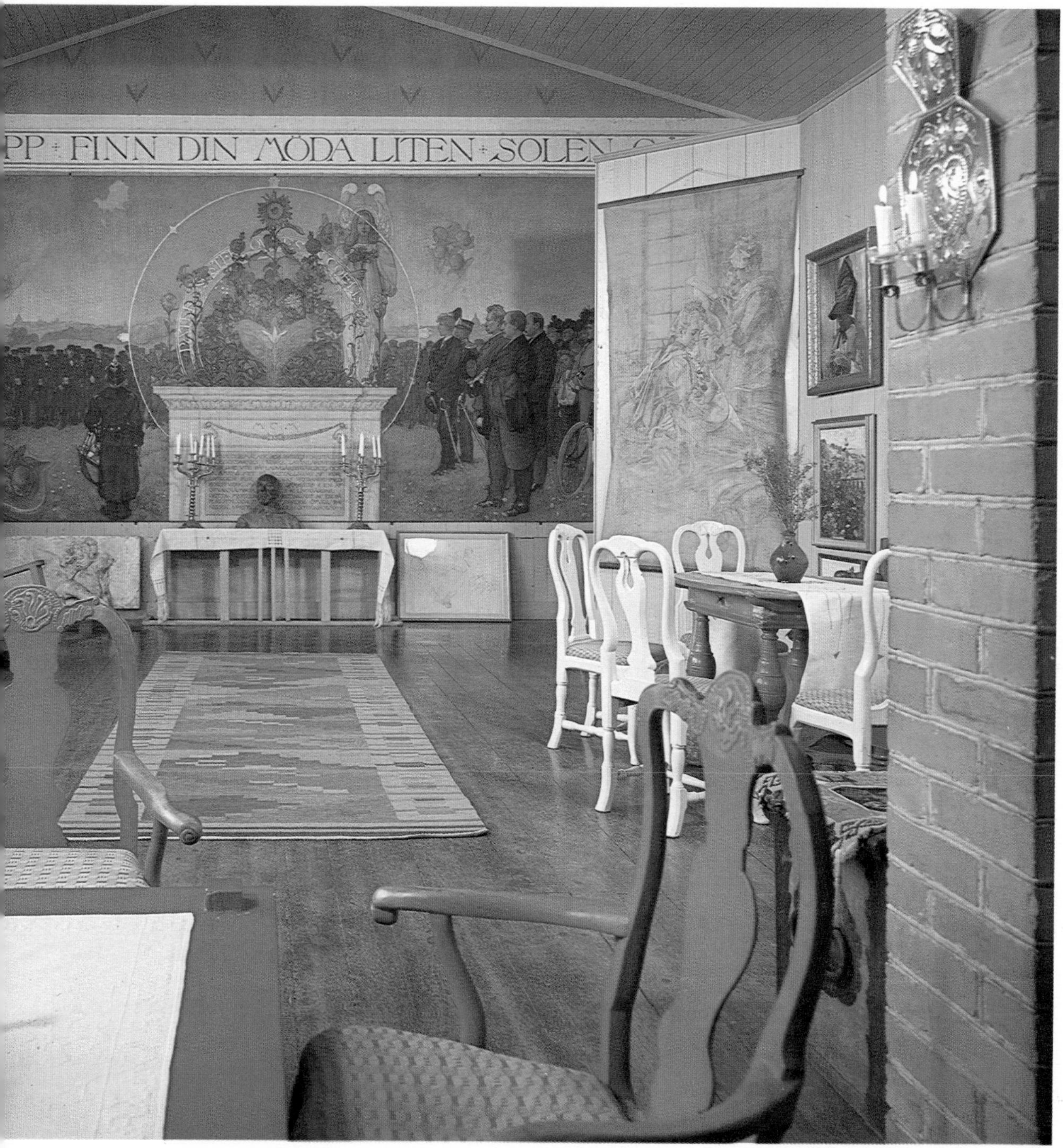
FINN DIN MÖDA LITEN
SOLEN

STEG · ÖKAD RO · MERA

The white—painted Rococo chairs played
an important part in the life of Carl Larsson, but not only as furniture. As an illustrator he worked very much with the 18th
Century and one comes to suspect that the
rhythmic lines of these very chairs have
inspired him. You only have to look at the
water—colour nearest the large open fireplace where a superiorly, almost hedoni-
cally depicted Rococo chair gives the painting its character. Against the wall is a so—
called turn—settle, which received its name
from the fact that the backrest can be
turned down towards the opposite side of
the settle by a simple turn of the hand. On
the wall are paintings by C.L. from different
periods: in the center the large "Mystery
of Life". In the Studio's open fireplace,
where a relief of Gustav Vasa—a cast from
Gripsholm—is inserted, we have placed a
toy stove from the Workshop. It is in full
working condition and can be used for
cooking. It was used frequently by the
Larsson children.

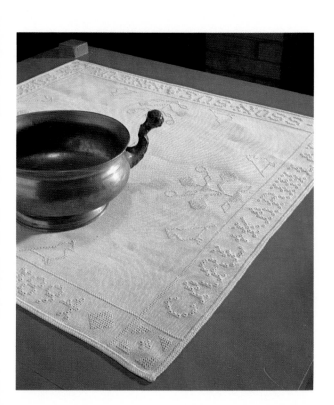

The West short–wall of the Studio is covered with a fine oak panelling, a Frisian work from the late 17th Century. It also allows for some cupboard and other storage space. Carl has described how he stumbled upon it in an antique shop, with only 600 crowns in his pocket: "The old wood was offered to me for 1200. I paid the sum immediately and wrote out my first and last draft for the remaining 600. Later it cost a pile of money to have them made. However it was a good bargain. Allow me to giggle at the thought of the Danish antique seller who didn't understand their real value." Part of that panelling is also in the Old Room. The sitting arrangement is in front of the warming fireplace around a sturdy red table designed by Karin. The magnificent 18th Century speaker's chair, with it high back-rest, protects from draughts. In the inset display cabinet on the back wall you get a glimpse of the fine collection of Lapp handiwork. It became popular after the exhibition of 1897. C.L. was, by the way, a friend of the Lappland king, Hjalmar Lundbohm, protector of the Lapps. In the smaller picture is a porridge bowl of pewter on one of Karin's cloths.

Weight and dignity lie over the fireplace corner of the Studio, which is in contrast with the lightness and modesty that characterizes Carl Larsson's Home in general. Partially this can be explained by the fact that C.L. came upon the stately Frisian panelling by chance and wanted very much to use it in the Sundborn home. But this more class—adhering interior also corresponds to a not so unimportant part of Carl Larsson's position. At the height of his career, he was the national painter, above others, and a highly thought of elevated figure in Swedish cultural life. His word weighed heavily in a long line of topics of current interest, and he was more than willing to express his brusque ideas. In this aspect the Studio was representative both regarding size and interior. But behind the grandeur panel was hidden the practical everyday arrangement. A small door to the right opens onto a narrow, steep stairway which leads to the summer rooms called the lower and upper Dovecote. Beside it is a door to an entrance hall with an outer door, on the North wall of the Studio. From this hallway you can also get to the previously—mentioned Bergman's room from Aspeboda.

Kitchen

Even today the kitchen of 1899 is essentially unchanged apart from the addition of the electric stove, the refrigerator and an improved drainage system, but the new inclusions are mostly movable and can be taken away. A plastic board lies over the old iron stove. The Kitchen, with its brownstained panelled walls, green shelves and red and white curtains, is genuinely cozy. In the middle of the floor stands a scrubbed table with benches, from the thirties. On the shelves are wonderful Höganäs ceramic pots which have been used frequently. Also in the kitchen is the cupboard moved from the Dingingroom, with its "Japanesque motifs" painted on the doors by C.L. During a certain period he was influenced by Japanese art, as were also his contemporaries, which the numerous Japanese woodcarvings at Sundborn testify to.

Maid's Chamber

It is said that the maids considered the kitchen the only "unspoiled" room in the whole house. Like the townsfolk, they also found it difficult to understand all the new—fangled things which the Larsson family brought into their peaceful world. The cook also preferred to sleep in the pleasant warmth of the kitchen rather than in the occasionally rather cold lodging, where she was assigned a bed. Karin's bed with its canopy was moved from the bedroom on the upper floor to the Maid's Chamber, where it stands today. The Maid's Chamber, with its walls of sunny yellow, brown tile oven and well—tuned textiles, however, is a rather unmatched bedroom.

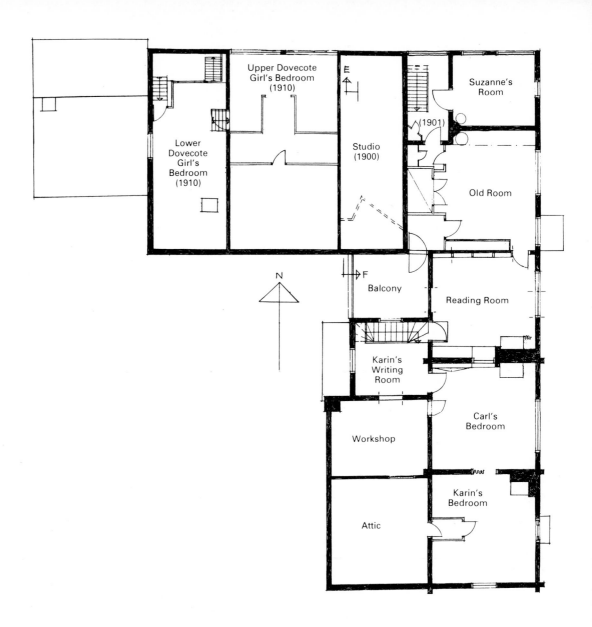

Lower
Dovecote
Girl's
Bedroom
(1910)

Upper Dovecote
Girl's Bedroom
(1910)

Studio
(1900)

E

(1901)

Suzanne's
Room

Old Room

N

Balcony

F

Reading Room

Karin's
Writing
Room

Carl's
Bedroom

Workshop

Karin's
Bedroom

Attic

Upper Level

Upper Hall

The narrow staircase with its white railing
leads us from the Entrance Hall to the
Upper Hall. This small space of about 7 m²
was used by Carl Larsson as a primitive
studio during the family's early stay at
Sundborn. Later on it became Karin's writing room. The ceiling is vaulted like a
ship's cabin, and the windows and doors
make it a very bright room. From here the
somewhat larger door to the right leads
into Carl's bedroom. The smaller door was
opened under a rebuilding phase and leads
to the Reading Room. The minimal wall
space is extensively used for paintings. In
the background you see works of their
friend, John Baur, and of Herman Norr-
man, who already as Carl Larsson's pupil
was prominent.

The scrubbed floor, the okra—yellow walls and the white-painted English—type balustrade, together with the white starched curtain, give the little hall its background atmosphere. Paintings are crowded all the way down the stairs, and the narrow shelf above the window is crammed with bric-a-brac. Otherwise the books on the shelves, mainly richly illustrated literature of art, play an important role in the living entirety. Carl Larsson used to praise himself for being Falun's greatest book purchaser. In front of the small—paned West window facing the yard stands one of the charming and practical flower stands which Karin had made—to—order.

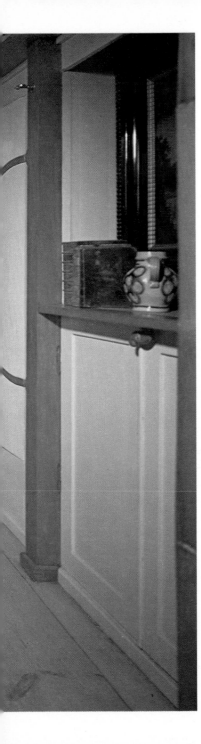

Carl's Bedroom

Carl Larsson's Bedroom is one of the most interesting rooms in the house, deviating completely from usual housing ideals. At the same time it shows most clearly how influenced he was by the then modern English interior decorating, which occasionally showed examples of canopied beds precisely of this free–standing type. Both bedrooms are, to a certain extent, parallels of the Diningroom and the Drawing–room. Even during the day Carl's bedroom is a twilight room which gets its light partially from Karin's South room. Despite its modest format this bedchamber is in a sense monumental and an expression of spontaneous self–consciousness on the part of the owner, a little room moulded with powerful and superior artistry. In the picture you are looking out towards the Upper Hall. Karin's textiles surround and cover the bed. To the right is the closed–off door to the Reading Room with a shelf for books and space for a painting. To the left of the open door is the shutter with a green creeper winding around it, covering the opening towards the earlier studio, now the Workshop.

This is what C.L. could see when he peeked down in the morning from his bedroom, into the Studio—Workshop. As from so many other places in this "open house", he could at the same time see out into the yard through the Workshop window. Arrangements with this type of peephole already existed during the Middle Ages, but here in Sundborn the variant is as independent as it is typical of the man of the house. C.L.'s bedroom has been rightfully called a complete work of art, an entity planned down to the minutest detail. This picture of the wall backing on the Reading Room and the door to the Upper Hall shows the unequalled daring and confidence of Carl Larsson's decorating.

Surely hygiene was rather primitive at the time. The garden table had to serve as a wash–stand when C.L. was shaving. So as not to need a window shade—such were not even found in the Sundborn home—coloured glass was set into the window. As already mentioned, Carl was not the only decorating champion in this peculiar home. Precisely in Carl's Bedroom, Karin has acted out her talent with superior confidence. The well–known Sundborn blanket on the bed and the so effectful bedcurtains, in their daring simplicity, show how compatible she was with her husband, even as an artist.

Indeed Carl Larsson slept in sole majesty in his bedchamber, as master of the house. But at the same time he had a near and intimate contact with his dear ones, in Karin's adjacent bedroom. There was no door that divided them, only the beautiful Flemish–weave drapery which Karin composed and made, one of the remarkable textiles of the Swedish art nouveau–epoch. Carl heard the breathing of his sleeping children next to him, and the small ones had to patter through pappa's room to get to the rest of the house. In the picture to the right you can see the practical shelf for evening reading and the nighttable. The lamp–cord was led through the foot of the bed so no one would trip on it. This is what C.L. wrote about his bedroom: "This is my room. It is supposed to be so healthy having the bed in the middle of the floor, but I didn't know about it when it was so decided... in my simple bed, on my straw mattress I sleep well and soundly, as a king in his *lit de parade.*"

Almost everything in the Carl Larsson bedchamber is attached to the wall and composed into a complete milieu. One of the few exceptions is the splendid Baroque chest which served as Karin's linen closet. As we have seen, Carl had a great interest in and a marked sense for the quality of old things. But he did not always treat them with exaggerated consideration and the piety which the now even more trimmed supply of older objects has taught us to feel. If C.L. found a nice surface to paint a flourish on, he did not deny himself the pleasure, and we can just accept and appreciate it when, as here he has created the most enticing full—figured portrait of his daughter Brita.

Karin's Bedroom

"… but look, in the other sleeping room you'll find the cherubs", wrote Carl Larsson, and we may very well call Karin's and the cherub's room one of the most loved ones in the Sundborn home. It underwent quite a radical treatment after the "aunts" left the house. The ceiling was torn down, the beams were built into boxes, the log ceiling was painted green and the walls were white—washed. The windows were made smaller. At the beginning of the 20th Century a practical wardrobe was built in the middle of the long—wall, which at the same time became a divider between the mother's and the children's beds. Within it there is a door leading to the attic, above the Workshop, which at times has been used as a summer room. Karin's bed, between the wardrobe and the wall, has almost acquired the character of a ship's berth.

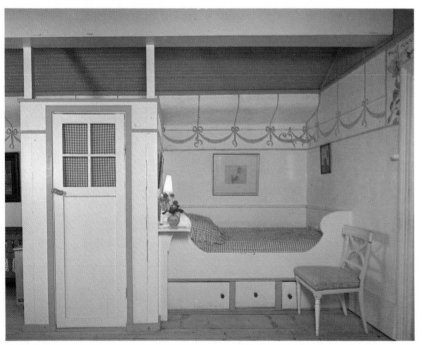

Karin's bedchamber was decorated for the first time in 1894, which is noticeable by the dedication which Carl painted over the doorway to his own bedroom, composed among flowers and flourishes, congratulations to Karin on her nameday. There is also a beautiful tile oven next to which stands a pot–cupboard with an original ceramic washbowl from Germany, manufactured by the potter in Oberammergau who played Christ in the passion plays between 1900–1910. On the left is one of the three portraits of Carl, which Karin always had beside her bed. The picture on the right, a closeup of the oven corner gives an idea of the fine colouristic interaction between the interior details and C.L.'s decor as well as Karin's door–hanging.

Two green children's beds still remain in Karin's and the cherub's sleeping room, ever since the beginning of the 20th Century, when the children moved away. Carl describes them as "two children's beds ingeniously made of pine chip, according to my wife's foolish suggestion". The idea of employing pine chip, used as a roof covering, for the beds was more ingenious than foolish and it is said that more than one visitor wished that beds of that type would have been for sale. The picture on the right shows how the window to the East was made smaller and set with coloured glass in order to prevent the Nordic morning sun from shining in too sharply on the small ones. In the foreground is Karin's dressing–table with its mahogany mirror at just the right angle and placed at exactly the right spot beneath the window.

Reading Room

"A sanctuary. Feel the quiet peace and the great solemnity. Holy words, beautiful hymns, serious and deep thoughts and the significant speech of righteousness, glad songs and sad entertaining tales, instructive experience and brilliant discoveries, the best works of art of all times reproduced, you will find all this and more still within the walls of this little cabin—like nook; I can almost say that whatever lofty and superior that the human spirit has accomplished, you can simply pick down for yourself from these bookshelves." The Reading Room, first a junk room, then a studio and livingroom, became a dear haunt for the tireless seeker of knowledge C.L. In an impressive way, he compensated at a mature age, for what he had missed of book—learning during his youth.

The Reading Room is small, only 4×4.5 metres, but appears much larger, loaded down as it is with books and art, literally from the floor to the ceiling. Even here Karin's arranging hand and fine taste have made their impression on the whole. The white woolen cloth on the table and the hanging lamp with its white shade and white knotted fringes effectively lighten–up the overwhelming dark impression. Only the border with its squares and the light, simplified motif in red and yellow on the short–walls are woven. She considered it meaningless to spend her time on the table surface, in such a demanding technique, that she spread a piece of white course home–woven cloth over it all. Technically simple and inartificially carpented shelves bear the book treasures. The picture below on the left shows the Northwest corner of the room with a mounting of Swedish handwriting styles, which underlines C.L.'s interest in the arts of lettering and calligraphy.

Through the small window panes of the Reading Room, set in lead, you catch a glimpse of tree tops and the stream flowing by in the East. The tide is quite strong here, since the water comes spurting directly from the turbines of the adjacent power plant. The picture is taken in late winter, while the inner window is still on—with reindeer lichen and immortelles between the frames—as well as the perpetal draught—edgings covering the crevices.

From the stairs and the Upper Hall the light shines in nicely on the portrait of daughter Kersti, painted on the mirror of the Reading Room door, which nearly always stands open or ajar. In general the doors in Carl Larsson's Home always stand open, here a closed door would be some what of a contradiction.

Old Room

From the Reading Room you come into the Old Room, which is the first one on the upper level of the new addition that joins the old house with the new Studio from 1899. C.L. writes: ''We call it so because everything old that I've acquired is collected and adapted to a whole and yet everything has a practical use. It is the actual guest room of the house... You'll find all kinds of things here, old Flemish paintings, cabinets, chests and tables from the 16th and 17th Centuries, a teatable with a painting by Elias Martin, a ceiling lantern from the era of Gustav III and Emil Högqvist's mirror from Framnäs, an old clock and old books, an unusual spice closet and a Rococo night–chair... that blue one, and old coins''. In the picture on the right is the mentioned spice closet, which of course has been repainted merrily and unforcedly in a way that would make a present–day restorer shiver.

The magnificent Frisian panel from the
17th Century, which we mentioned in refer-
ence to the Studio, was even enough for
the decoration of the Old Room. Behind
the panelling you will find the already familiar built–in bed "… a bed as a bed should
be…" according to C.L. A wall–hanging
designed by Gustaf Fjaestod can be
glimpsed behind the bed, and as a pleasing
contrast Karin's Sundborn blanket, designed to be woven and sold by women of
the village skilled in weaving. On the inside
of the doors are the names of a good many
of the more or less famous or closer or
more distant acquaintances who have visit-
ed the Larsson home. The high backrest of
the blue chair is upholstered with a Gobe-
lin tapestry by Karin. On the table is a
self–portrait of C.L. Self–searching with a
clown–like doll, which can still be found in
the house.

The picture on the facing page shows the earlier–mentioned blue armchair in its entirety. You see that Karin tried to make the pattern fit the slight museum–like character of the room. The Old Room differs quite considerably from the rest of the house. Its somewhat heavy pomp is not Carl Larssonish in the same sense as the other decorating and cannot be credited the same cultural–historical value as the other rooms, let be that it is more lavishly furnished from an economic viewpoint. If C.L. let the tile oven in the Drawing–room bloom up to the ceiling, then Karin has supplemented the single–coloured green of the tile oven with "frills" on the stone slab in front of the fire–opening. On the ceiling C.L. himself painted several sayings, this one is: "Truly old is only that which is eternally young."

Suzanne's Room

The eldest daughter Suzanne's room was decorated in connection with the earlier—mentioned addition. You get there either through a passageway from the Old Room or from downstairs by a steep staircase to the right of the kitchen entrance, which is next to the Studio's white—washed, earlier outer wall towards the East. On the opposite side of the stairs is an English—type slatwork painted white. Suzanne's Room is small and bright with plastered walls and green woodworking which picks up the colour of the likewise green tile oven. In the picture on the left you see the oven as well as the mentioned plastered studio wall and stair—railing. Over the door is a flower creeper painted by Suzanne in Carl's style. In the picture to the right you catch a glimpse of the decoration motif as well as a Gustavian mirror and the white curtains hung from cloth loops, Karin's typical arrangement.

Acknowledgements

The author of the texts in this book, since his childhood and youth, has enjoyed the great advantage of being in touch with Carl Larsson's Home and the people who made it and still keep it alive. Its spirit is incomparable. If anywhere, the people and the milieu are joined in an indissoluable alliance in this home.

The factual details in this volume are taken from many sources, mostly from Carl Larsson's books, articles and letters, which, along with his wife Karin's letters, were later presented in such an exemplary way by Axel Frieburg in his simultaneously penetrating, tactful and intimate book, *Karin.*

I have received information about the buildings and their interior decoration through the kindness of Carl Larsson's great granddaughter, the architect Anita Nordström who, with her colleague Britt-Marie Salmén, undertook a precise measuring of the house, described its details and further presented a series of basic information about the house, seen from an architectural and milieu–historical view, for her thesis at the School of Technology, Stockholm, in 1967–1968. Both floor plans are taken from that work.

Another important source has been Eva von Zweigbergk's excellent book, *At Home with the Carl Larssons,* that important first try to place Little Hyttnäs into a cultural–historical framework.

The author would also like to thank the Family Society through its chairman, Professor Stig Ranström, on the part of the photographer and himself for his acceding to let us work at Carl Larsson's Home, and to Mrs. Greta Hytte for her invaluable practical contribution during our stays at Sundborn. We would also like to express our thankfulness to the members of the family society who helped us by examining the text and the pictures.